Self Guided Tour:
Abolitionists of Plymouth

Andrea M. Daly

Copyright © 2015 Andrea Daly

ISBN: 978-1-63263-402-3

All rights reserved. No part of this publication may be reproduced, stored in a retrieval system, or transmitted in any form or by any means, electronic, mechanical, recording or otherwise, without the prior written permission of the author.

Published by BookLocker.com, Inc., Bradenton, Florida.

Printed on acid-free paper.

BookLocker.com, Inc.
2015

First Edition

Acknowledgments

When I began researching for this book, my interests were inspired by listening to my grandmother's tales of growing up in Plymouth and by my own experiences. I am the fifth generation living in Plymouth on my maternal side of my family. I was a researcher in the Plymouth Public Library's History Room and a member of their Oral History Project; a docent for a couple of the local historical houses; a historical tour guide for Plymouth tourism; and an avid participant in the preservation of history for the local Antiquarian Society. All my experiences helped me find the diamond in the rough, the abolitionists of Plymouth.

As a docent in Plymouth's historic homes, I unraveled the owners' lives in their letters with stories of Plymouth I never learned as a school-aged child. The political figures, writers, seafarers, and unique individuals who lived in Plymouth centuries ago always fascinated me. I was intrigued with the unknown or lost history of people who were significant in making a change in 19th century Plymouth, at the time a remote town.

It's easy to misunderstand my town's complete history when it's been monopolized with the Landing of the Pilgrims and the early colonial era. I immersed myself reading books and articles of local 19th century authors, homeopathic women doctors, founders of local industries and others. I am a fifth generation of Plymouth descendents on my maternal side.

Most of my articles were found in forgotten files or book shelves at Smith College, Harvard University, on microfiche at the Plymouth Public Library, and at Pilgrim Hall Museum. Internet access made it easier to locate period books all over the world. Computers can be helpful and also track keywords, and once I started doing my research, I noted more information springing up on my main character, Abby Morton Diaz.

After years of doing my own historical tours on foot, in and out of costume, I put together this walking tour narrative, focused in part on

Andrea M. Daly

Abby the "Silver Tongued Prophetess," I hope my interests in preserving these stories of local history will inspire you to walk the tour.

    A special thanks to S. Mabell Bates of the Maxwell Library at Bridgewater State University; Smith College's Sophia Collection Librarians; Radcliffe's Reference Librarians; Photograph Coordinator at Radcliffe's Schlesinger Library, Marie-Helene Gold; Peggy Baker, Director/Curator of Pilgrim Hall Museum; Librarian Bev Ness at the Plymouth Public Library; Plymouth's Oak Hills Cemetery Supervisor, Bradford Bartlett; the Belmont Cemetery's Supervisor; Dr. Donna Curtin, Director/Curator of the Antiquarian Society and always, my many supportive family members and friends.

Andrea M. Daly
Plymouth, Massachusetts

Introduction

Who were the abolitionists? In 19th century Plymouth Massachusetts, they were people who banded together to fight for the freedom of black slaves. This booklet will teach you about abolitionists who lived and visited Plymouth.

After years of researching local history, I came across an interesting article named, "Anti-Slavery Times in Plymouth", by Abigail Morton Diaz. I found this article hidden in the archives of Pilgrim Hall Museum, a nationally known museum of Pilgrim history, not the place one would expect to find 19th century materials. Abigail's youthful activities as "secretary" for a juvenile abolitionist group in Plymouth made her an eyewitness to the town's local anti-slavery movement; her lineage connected her to Plymouth's early history. She was a direct descent of Pilgrim Ephraim Morton whose youngest brother Nathaniel was Secretary of Pilgrim Colony. Even though the museum had only one article by Abigail Morton Diaz, this key source allowed me to research other avenues and discover more information about this abolitionist and others in the 19th century.

Abigail Morton was the daughter of Ichabod and Patty (Cole-Weston) Morton. Patty Morton died when Abigail was only seven years old. Her father remarried to Betsey Holbrook. Five brothers soon came from that marriage. Abigail was raised by a father who was very religious, coupled with high standards for human kindness and a belief in the betterment of all mankind. Abigail learned that even though her father's values were highly admired by some, they did not reflect all who lived in her hometown.

The majority of people in Plymouth were descendants of English settlers, and at first did not look kindly upon the abolitionist cause. Desire Harlow was one of the young abolitionists in town; her obituary and an article written by W.L. Garrison spoke of her courage as a watchman for anti-slavery meetings. Following one such meeting, the sign to the anti-slavery reading room was tarred.

Abigail was a special person because she learned to rise above those who tried to keep her from learning more. Whenever things looked dark and the struggle was harder, it gave Abigail a reason to do more and be heard. Abby married Manuel Diaz, a man from Cuba. She met him when teaching at the Transcendentalist utopian community at Brook Farm. She attended higher education and was in the first graduating class at the Normal School in Bridgewater, later known as Bridgewater State College. Later she gave lectures, taught dance as well as school for young children, was a co-founder of the Women's Educational and Industrial Union in Boston, and authored children's literature and numerous articles, including religious essays for the Christian Science founded by Mary Baker. Eddy.

If you choose to walk this Abolitionist Tour, you will have the opportunity of mirroring their footsteps in the dirt paths from well over a hundred years ago. Addresses are provided to allow you to GPS the locations.

You will see abolitionists' homes, the sites where they worshipped, listened to lectures and learned about other abolitionist friends who frequented Plymouth. The most popular site for anti-slavery lectures was the home of Bourne Spooner in North Plymouth. Spooner was a very religious man, an industrialist and quite a story teller, admirably mentioned by all who were welcomed into his home. His interest, wealth and wit, along with the efforts of the Morton family, appeared to be the backbone of the Anti-Slavery Society in Plymouth.

This booklet gives you a lot of information where you may see sites from this period. Read the timeline of Abigail Morton Diaz and maybe purchase one of the children's books which she illustrated and authored. Local newspaper obituaries collected on microfiche in the Plymouth Public Library reveal her dedication as an activist.

Today, people are still fighting for their freedom in other parts of the world and on our own soil. Abolitionist work will go on as long as people are being kept as slaves by other people. Will slavery ever end? What have we learned from history, from past attempts to end slavery? Can brotherhood and sisterhood be strong enough to abolish slavery everywhere? Can we cut through political, religious, ethnic and tribal

Self Guided Tour: Abolitionists of Plymouth

barriers which keep slavery alive? Nearly two hundred years ago, the focus was on freeing black slaves. Today we still, hear the cry for freedom and human compassion around the world.

Abby Morton Diaz

Photo: Courtesy of The Plymouth Antiquarian Society

Contents

THE LIFE OF ABBY MORTON DIAZ 1
   FAMILY AND FRIENDS 1

PLYMOUTH'S ABOLITION TOUR 15
   SITE 1: EPHRAIM HARLOW'S HOMESTEAD, CIRCA 1800 3 ROBINSON STREET, PLYMOUTH CENTER 15
   SITE 2: ROBINSON SOCIETY CHURCH, CIRCA 1830 MARKET STREET EXTENSION 16
   SITE 3: TRAINING GREEN & THE CIVIL WAR MONUMENT SANDWICH STREET, RTE. 3A AND PLEASANT STREET 17
   SITE 4: THE THIRD CONGREGATIONAL SOCIETY, CIRCA 1801. CRAIG/MACAFERRI RESIDENCE, CIRCA 1906 37 PLEASANT STREET 18
   SITE 5: THE WELLINGSLEY SCHOOL HOUSE, CIRCA 1815. JABEZ CORNER, BEHIND BRADFORD LIQUOR STORE 19
   SITE 6: EDWIN MORTON'S HOMESTEAD, CIRCA 1791 218 SANDWICH STREET 21
   SITE 7: ICHABOD MORTON'S HOMESTEAD, CIRCA 1750 212 SANDWICH STREET 22
   SITE 8: THE STEPHEN'S HOMESTEAD, CIRCA 1854 STEPHEN'S LANE (ON THE SHORE) 24
   SITE 9: THE FIRST BAPTIST CHURCH, CIRCA 1822-61. SPRING LANE, PLYMOUTH 29
   SITE 10: THE SHERMAN BUILDING, CIRCA 1887 MAIN STREET, LYMOUTH CENTER 30
   SITE 11: NORTH STREET, PLYMOUTH CENTER 32
   SITE 12: THE MAYFLOWER SOCIETY HOUSE, CIRCA 1756 3 WINSLOW STREET 36
   SITE 13: THE OLD COLONY CLUB HOUSE 25 COURT STREET, PLYMOUTH CENTER 37

SITE 14: CLARK'S ISLAND, PLYMOUTH BAY 38
SITE 15: THE LYLE FAMILY HOMESTEAD, CIRCA EARLY18THC. 174
   COURT STREET, PLYMOUTH\ 40
SITE 16: BOURNE SPOONER'S HOMESTEAD, CIRCA 1824 373 COURT
   STREET, PLYMOUTH 41

THE ANTI-SLAVERY ALPHABET 43

SUGGESTED READING 45

BOOKS BY ABIGAIL MORTON DIAZ 47

TIME LINE DURING THE LIFE OF ABIGAIL MORTON DIAZ 49

*"The seed of anti-slavery fell in Plymouth on sandy soil, but watered
By heavenly dew, it soon took root and broke through the conservative
Crust which under the influence of the commercial and financial
interests of
Town, for a time obstructed its growth."*

– Wm. T. Davis

The Life of Abby Morton Diaz
Family and Friends

Abby was born in Plymouth, Massachusetts on November 22, 1821. She was the first born to Ichabod and Patty (Weston) Morton. Abby was given the name Abigail but preferred the nickname Abby early in life. She was a spirited child and became a laborer for mankind at a very young age. I use the name laborer to describe Abby for her life work was usually behind the scenes and not as a lecturer for the abolitionist circuits.

From the young age of four into adulthood, Abby Morton helped the Fragment Society. This Society had members collect cast off clothing and food for those in need. Most important were the visits to the friendless. Abby's Aunt Sally (Sarah Morton) Stephens (Ichabod's sister) was a President of the Fragment Society. Their mission was to help those in need locally. This society is still active in Plymouth.

There is no question about Abby's dedication as an abolitionist. However, she also was an advocate for social change, who supported the betterment of education for children, and later equal rights for women on the job and in politics. Throughout Abby's life, her mission was to obtain a better life for all.

When she was about eight years old, some of Abby's friends began a Juvenile Anti-Slavery Society in 1829-30. They elected Abby as their Secretary. My research documents other young girls of Plymouth who were involved with the Juvenile Anti-Slavery Society. The five Harlow sisters from Robinson Street were members: Jane, Hannah, Ruth, Zilpha and Desire; also Julia Kendall, Helen Morton, and Sarah Stephens. Abby's cousins Helen Morton and Sarah Stephens also supported the expansion of rights, including suffrage, for women. Julia Kendall was the daughter of the Reverend Kendall of Plymouth's First Church. Today the First Church is known as the Unitarian Church in Town Square at the foot of Burial Hill. The basement of the First Church was used for the lectures and fairs to raise money for numerous causes. Julia was also a classmate of Abby and Desire Harlow during their formal educational years at the Bridgewater Normal School. Reverend Kendall supported numerous lectures in the basement of his church; Ralph Waldo Emerson was a regular lecturer there. Today the lower activity hall is named for Reverend Kendall – Kendall Hall.

There may have been other juvenile anti-slavery members not uncovered by my research. However, local families or descendants may find more information on abolitionists in their attics and pass on such treasures.

In her writing, Abby described the origins of Plymouth's Anti-Slavery Society, inaugurated in her Aunt Phebe (Stephens) Cotton's home. The Society had separate male and female branches; this first meeting may have been the beginning of the Female Anti-Slavery Society in Plymouth. Abby recollected her cousin Sarah Stephens was its Secretary. The men's Anti-Slavery Society, "The Old Colony Anti-Slavery Society," started around the same time, too, according to the memories of Sarah Stephens. Sarah spoke proudly about her father, Lemuel Stephens, being the local spirit for organizing the Anti-Slavery Society. Sarah was a Morton cousin; her mother was Abby's Aunt Sally (Morton) Stephens.

There were uneasy feelings amongst townspeople who were prejudiced and prone to favor slavery due to their industrial relations with the Southern plantation owners. For women to support black men in having equal rights with white men was viewed as a disgrace to their English heritage. The English were afraid to "taint their blood lines" with any immigrant in the town of Plymouth. However, there were always individuals who took a broader, less prejudiced view of those of different races and backgrounds than their own, and sought to befriend or assist them.

Advertisements of the men's Old Colony Anti-Slavery Meetings were often listed in the local newspaper but rarely the women's meetings. Those meetings were private, word of mouth, mainly so that they could get their work done and not be interrupted by a hateful mob. Their involvement was shown through the organizing of anti-slavery fairs and progressive lectures. The money collected benefitted the anti-slavery cause. The women organized an anti-slavery room in the town. According to local 19th century historian William T. Davis, it was located in the Sherman Building on Main Street. The original wooden building no longer survives, but the brick building that replaced it bears a stone plaque with its 1887 date of construction. The numbers are engraved on the face at the top of the building.

Abby mentioned how the eldest Harlow sisters maintained the reading room which was devoted to anti-slavery literature. The society members, especially eldest sister Ruth Harlow, made the room a social center to benefit the cause. Abby and her friends were delighted when a new *Liberator* newspaper arrived and was added to the reading room literature. Every time anti-slavery agents lectured, it was published in the *Liberator*. Learning about new converts, the next gatherings, fairs, or new speakers was all available in the *Liberator*! Uncle Edwin Morton never disappointed the girls by bringing home the *Liberator* from his travels into Boston.

Abby did not write about her mother, Patty Weston, who grew up on North Street. Patty descended from the Cole family, which is how Cole's Hill got its name. The hill is the one which faces the ocean and overlooks the 1620 Plymouth Rock. Abby's grandmother was Patty Cole who married Coomer Weston. They made their home in the Weston family block on North Street. This street is on the second oldest street in Plymouth from the landing of the Pilgrims in 1620. North Street had previous names. Today the "Weston Block" is seen as the row of houses (#8-12); Patty and Coomer's home was 12 North Street. Various Weston relations occupied the houses, which were attached; the women did not need to go outside in bad weather but could visit via passages between each house.

Abby's grandmother was known as Ma'am Weston to many residents in the early 19th century. Ma'am Weston ran an infant school, also known as a Dame School, in her home. She was kindly remembered by two of her students who became writers of local history, William T. Davis and Laura Russell. Davis grew up in the north corner house on Cole's Hill.

Today, the childhood home of William T. Davis is the site of condominiums; prior to that it was the Plymouth National Wax Museum and earlier the Plymouth Rock Hotel. Davis' grandfather planted the linden tree which stood in the north corner of Cole's Hill and grew to massive size. The tree was cut down when the condominiums were built. In an old local news article, I found the tree was nicknamed "The Spoon Holder." Many lovers were caught "spooning" under its shade.

William T. Davis was very involved with the town and its people. Davis' memoirs depict the history of the town of Plymouth. His writings are vital for Plymouth researchers. Laura Russell was another local writer and grew up at 26 North Street. Laura's mother was Deborah Spooner, a sister to abolitionist Bourne Spooner. He founded the Cordage Company in 1824. It was cause for rejoicing for local abolitionists when Bourne became a convert to the cause; he later became President of The Old Colony Anti-Slavery Society.

The Russell family was known for a repeated preference for the use of the name John. The only way to talk about the men without confusion was to refer to their nicknames. Laura's father was Deep Water John, who followed family tradition and sailed the seven seas. Laura is known for her book "Laura Russell Remembers", another great source of local light hearted history regarding the 19th century.

Abby's maternal grandfather, Coomer Weston, was well known in town as a seaman. He also was a member of Plymouth's first organized militia, "The Standish Guards." When he was just 32 years old, his ship was wrecked off the shores of Nantucket. He died. This tragic loss of Abby's grandfather Coomer may be the reason why her grandmother Weston opened a Dame School. Mrs. Weston had to provide for her four children. Abby's mother, Patty, was the oldest of her siblings and died in her thirties like her father. She was only 36 years of age. Abby was not quite six years old when her mother died on August 2, 1827.

Throughout Abby's life, she was interested in her father's mission of making life better for her and all of mankind. Abby loved people and studied them carefully. Her children's books express her candid portrayals of people, children and life. Later her interests in writing expanded in relation with women's rights and the laborers or lecturers for the anti-slavery cause.

Abby's father, Ichabod Morton grew up on the property which was granted to the Morton family in 1623. The property was in the Wellingsley area of town. Ichabod descended from George and Juliana

(Southworth) Morton who came to Plymouth in the ship Ann in 1623. Ichabod's direct descent is from the youngest child Ephraim who was born on the seas to Plymouth. (See Family Chart). Ephraim's older brother Nathaniel followed his father's footsteps in being the Secretary of the early Plimoth Plantation.

Abby had a brother Nathaniel as well. He was younger than she and turned out to be very successful and stayed living in Plymouth. He donated a portion of his land to build a school, known today as the Nathaniel Morton School on Lincoln Street. He also donated the land which once belonged to Benjamin Watson. The land was famously known as "The Old Colony Nurseries." Today, downsized, the land is known as Morton Park. This land was known to be surveyed by Henry David Thoreau of Concord. The Concord Poets were very friendly with the Watson family and many other families in Plymouth due to their religious, agricultural, literary and connection with Harvard College. These families helped form Plymouth's Literary Society. The Lyceum Hall or any other available hall had many well known men and women come to Plymouth to lecture.

Abby's father, Ichabod, is listed as a merchant in town records. He began building ships in his teens. At the age of 17 he was supervising the building of ships. Throughout the 19th century, with the exception of the Embargo Act, Plymouth's waterfront had a very active port with ships arriving and departing. The Old Colony Memorial newspaper had a "Mariner Journal" which always posted the arrivals, departures and hardships of vessels in connection to Plymouth's town wharves. Ichabod was a highly respected man in the town of Plymouth. He was known for his involvement in education, temperance, the anti-slavery movement, transcendentalism and was a devout religious man. His love for mankind was mirrored by his daughter and later by his sons. Ichabod's involvement in Abby's life is reflected in many of her choices. His love for education allowed him to work with Horace Mann, first Secretary of Education in Massachusetts. They were instrumental in building the Normal School in Bridgewater and many others. This school was one of the first to educate women as well as men for teaching.

Abby attended its first class in 1840. Abby was not alone. Her dear friend and abolitionist, Desire Harlow attended the first class at the Normal School in Bridgewater.

It was through Ichabod's undying interest in the anti-slavery movement and his religious foundation and encounter – "a vision" – for peace and equality amongst mankind which compelled Abby to support his humanitarian devotion. "The Anti-Slavery Society was formed by the Robinson Society on the evening of July 4th, Eighteen Hundred and Thirty Five.," (quote by William T. Davis' Memoirs of an Octogenarian). Her support of the women's suffrage movement began when she helped incorporate the Women's Educational and Industrial Union in 1880. Dr. Harriet Clisby inspired Abby to help women shortly after Abby had moved to Belmont, Massachusetts for her son Roberto. Dr. Harriet Clisby, Arvilla B. Haynes, Melissa Chamberlin, Sarah E. Eaton, Sarah E. Cotting, Elizabeth G. Gay and Abby M. Diaz formed a corporation under the name of the "Women's Educational and Industrial Union." Their purpose was to increase fellowship amongst women and promote their educational, industrial and social advancement. Abby lead a very interesting life, full of fellowship and inspiration.

Her father's second marriage to Betsey Holbrook of Plymouth resulted in five Morton sons; George E. 1829, Nathaniel 1831, Ichabod 1833, Austin 1834, and Howard 1836. Ichabod bought the house on Sandwich Street for his second bride. This home is known today as "The Hobshole Condominiums." It was a "safe house" for fugitive slaves and meeting place for many abolitionists. Ichabod was not only an abolitionist supporter; he moved into the utopian community, Brook Farm, with other family members and fellow reformers. During 1843, Abby's father had been a supporter of Ralph Waldo Emerson's free thinking community – where one could improve on the social forms of life, where all members stood equal by respecting each other's occupation and helping each other. Abby's father and his brother Edwin had intended to live at Brook Farm with their young families but, two months after building their 21 room "Pilgrim House" they left the community.

They returned to Plymouth to their Sandwich Street homes for they had reservations about the survival of Emerson's prime idea of equality within the Brook Farm community. After Abby's father's and uncle's departure from Brook Farm, she stayed on to teach at the community's Infant School.

She must have been overwhelmed with excitement with the scholars that came to lecture, teach or partake in one of the plays at Brook Farm. It was during her time at Brook Farm that Abby met her husband Manuel Diaz at a picnic, a boat party gathering. He was from Cuba and came to Boston as a student.

Plymouth town records show that Abby bought a piece of land with her husband Manuel which sat behind her father's homestead closer to the shore. Their homestead is no longer standing. I wonder if the barn on the property was converted into their home. Was it the cabin that the slave stealer, Jonathan Walker, found refuge in for his family in 1851?

With the lack of original 19th century Plymouth records, secondary sources for this proof were inconclusive. In his book, Jonathan Walker spoke about being in Plymouth in a rustic cabin. Ichabod's property could have suited this description of Jonathan's. The Morton home was where some of the anti-slavery meetings were held or philosophical conversations were carried on with Bronson Alcott of Concord. Many of Ichabod's relatives were members of the Anti-Slavery Society, and formed a vigorous minority in town.

Abby's father and her uncles Edwin Morton and Lemuel Stephens were agents for the Anti-Slavery Society. Also noted agents for the anti-slavery movement were friends Ephraim Harlow, Rev. Samuel J. May and Lemuel's father William. Lemuel Stephens married Abby's paternal aunt Sarah, known as Aunt Sally. The Stephens family lived in a waterfront area referred to as "down the lane," today known as Stephen's Lane. Both the Morton and Stephens estates had their own wharves due to their professions as merchants and ship builders.

Abby had broadly tolerant views of humanity and equality, and when Manuel Diaz asked her to marry him, she agreed, despite their differing ethnicities. The couple returned to Plymouth to live. Though the Mortons may not have been troubled by the marriage, not everyone in town agreed. There were divisions between people of different ethnic backgrounds and religions which were rarely crossed in Abby's youth, and which persisted for many generations in Plymouth.

In town records, Miss Abby Morton of Plymouth and Mr. Manuel A. Diaz of Havana recorded their intentions of marriage on September 19th, 1845. Her cousin Sarah Stephens and Mr. Charles Burton of Pittsburgh, Pennsylvania, also recorded their marriage intentions on the same day. Sarah met Mr. Burton through her brother Edward. Burton began teaching in Plymouth and later became Superintendent of Plymouth schools. Abby and her cousin Sarah married a day apart in October of 1845. Abby Morton and Manuel Diaz married on the 6th of October and Sarah Stephens and Charles Burton married on the 5th of October.

I'm not certain what profession Manuel followed in Plymouth for it is not recorded. In the archives in the Registry of Deeds, Book 253, on Sept. 10, 1850, Manuel obtained a loan of $300 from the Plymouth Savings Bank. He and Abby bought land from John Bartlett. The land contained a barn with more or less of one and three quarter acres. This land was located east of her father's home as recorded in Book 243, page 189: in 1852, Abby gave up her dowry to buy land with Manuel, and legalized it on January 9. That same year, in Book 248, page 238, Ichabod gave Manuel $600 to free him from debt. So it's clear Manuel was still living in Plymouth up until 1852.

As I mentioned earlier, Sarah Stephens was as much a part of the anti-slavery movement as Abby. The women's memories of their 30-year plight to abolish slavery are found in the article written by Abigail Morton Diaz, "Antislavery Times In Plymouth." The timeline provided will not only give you places where Abby attended Anti-Slavery Meetings, but sites abolitionist speakers who came to Plymouth appeared. These speakers included William Lloyd Garrison (m. Eliza Benson), Rev. Samuel J. May (wife was sister to Bronson Alcott and a known general agent and corresponding secretary for the Massachusetts Anti-Slavery Society), Lydia Maria Child, Henry B. Stanton (wife Cady) Parker Pillsbury, Ralph Waldo Emerson (m. 2nd Lydia Jackson of Plymouth), Stephen Foster(married Abby Kelly), Frederick Douglass, William Wells Brown, William and Ellen Craft, Abby

Folsom, George Thompson (from England), Theodore Parker, Theodore Weld (m. Angelina Griminske), Edmund Quincy, Sallie Holley (of Pennsylvania), Horace Mann, Wendell Phillips, Whittier (a poet), Mary Grew (of Pennsylvania), Charles A. Dana, George W. Curtis, Benjamin Drew (taught in Boston) and Frederick Law Olmstead (father of national acclaimed architect).

I have tried to include all the speakers Abby would have heard in or outside of Plymouth. During her early days laboring for the emancipation of black slaves, Abby and her friends would attend anti-slavery lectures in any weather. Her dedication to this cause was remarkable and truly shows the strong character these women maintained.

A watch guard for anti-slavery meetings was always provided by the Juvenile Anti-Slavery Society in Plymouth. There were incidents of mobs disapproving of their gatherings so various meeting places had to be secured to avoid unwelcome attention. An anti-slavery reading room was kept in the Sherman Block on Main Street. As a building on the trail, this building was on the west side of Main Street according to the memoirs of William T. Davis. Abby talked about their Anti-Slavery Reading Room sign being tarred. This act was exciting for the girls to witness for their purpose was raising attention! This young group of abolitionists also assisted in passing out literature in town, raising money in fairs, securing safe places for meetings, educating the public on anti-slavery issues and assisting in writing to Congress to support the abolition of slavery.

Abby spoke of how important moral and constitutional principles were for the abolition of slavery. She also emphasized strong moral character in all her books in children's literature. She was a co-founder and strong supporter of the Women's Educational and Industrial Union in Boston.

Abby gave her first lecture about strong characters of children needed in schools in Philadelphia. This lecture started Abby on a circuit of speaking to women's groups on her famous series of "Household Talks."

In this pamphlet, there will be some duplication of information on the walking tour due to the houses affiliated with certain people.

Bourne Spooner

The Plymouth County Anti Slavery Society,

In view of the contemplated departure of GEORGE THOMPSON Esq.M.P. by the steamer for England, on the 17th inst., would invite the friends of Impartial Liberty, and the public generally, to a farewell meeting. At Leyden Hall in this town, on Thursday (this) evening June 12th. Addresses may be expected from Messrs GARRISON, QUINCY, PHILLIPS and others, and from that veterans of Human Rights, GEORGE THOMPSON. BOURNE SPOONER –Pres't.

H.H. BRIGHAM—Sec. (June 12 1851 OCM)

OCM – OLD Colony Memorial – local newspaper

To begin the tour find the entrance of Brewster Gardens across from the John Carver Inn.

Self Guided Tour: Abolitionists of Plymouth

Lemuel Stephens - Courtesy of The Plymouth Antiquarian Society

Sally Morton Stephens (spouse of Lemuel Stephens)

Courtesy of The Plymouth Antiquarian Society

Plymouth's Abolition Tour

Site 1:
Ephraim Harlow's Homestead, circa 1800
3 Robinson Street, Plymouth Center

Ephraim's backyard encompassed the land where the entrance to Brewster Garden is today. He donated this piece of property for the building of The Robinson Society's Church.

This was the home of abolitionist Ephraim Harlow (Feb. 23, 1770- Dec.15, 1858) and his two families. Ephraim was first married to Jerusha Doten, who died young in 1805. They had four children: Jerusha, Ephraim, Thomas and Jabez. Ephraim then married Ruth Sturtevant of Carver and had five daughters: Jane (m. Atwood L. Drew), Hannah (m. George Adams), Ruth, (spinster, d. 1893), Zilpha (m. Nathaniel Bourne Spooner) and Desire, who died young (d. 1848) from contracting typhus.

Members of Ephraim's second family were known abolitionists in Plymouth. His daughter's husbands were noted so you can see how well connected this family became within the town. The most poignant piece of literature which associated Desire Harlow as a true abolitionist was in her obituary found in the abolitionist newspaper, *The Liberator*.

The article read, "never a spirit more pure, a friend more interested, an advocate more faithful, a laborer more active and untiring, a witness more direct, a watchman more vigilant, than the deceased." Desire had just graduated from Bridgewater's Normal School, aka Bridgewater State University. She landed a job in Boston at the Asylum for the Blind

Site 2:
Robinson Society Church, circa 1830
Market Street Extension

Today, the site is part of Brewster Garden, owned by the Town of Plymouth. Ephraim Harlow's property and was once his backyard. (Site 1). This church looked like a one room school house with a bell in its front tower. In 1830, Ephraim Harlow donated his property for the construction of the Robinson Society Church

The last business held here was a sawmill owned by Carroll Howland. The Redevelopment Authority razed this building in the 1970's along with many other old buildings as part of an urban renewal project in the area, hence Brewster Garden was established.

Members of this church had renounced themselves from the Third Congregational Church. Mr. Harlow was one of these members who disassociated himself with the Third Congregational Church due to a disagreement of pastoral authority with Pastor Rev. Frederick Freeman.

This was the same Reverend Freeman who moved to Sandwich, Massachusetts and whose family portraits are exhibited in the Sandwich Glass Museum.

The Robinson Society Church became a crucial meeting place for the town's abolitionists. The Dedication Sermon for the Robinson Congregational House of Worship was on July 6, 1831. Unfortunately, this church was used for only 21 years after its erection by its members. There seemed to be a lot of disagreement with pastors for early society members. Some members had belonged to the First Church in Town Square. Later to the Third Congregational Church overlooking the Training Green then, In 1852 Robinson Society members reorganized with local congregational members and built the "Church of the Pilgrimage" which still stands in Town Square.

This church became a crucial meeting place for the anti-slavery meetings and lectures. It was here and at several local private homes which Desire Harlow and other young abolitionists would stand watch to report any sign of threat to the on-going meeting.

* **Face south to walk up Pleasant Street**

Site 3:
Training Green & the Civil War Monument
Sandwich Street, Rte. 3A and Pleasant Street

Just south of town center lies this Training Green which was formally designed in 1889 by Frederick Law Olmstead, Jr. Mr. Olmstead is well known for his architectural designs. This particular project is known as Blueprint Job #1151. The job cost the town $1,200.

The Training Green's history can be traced to the land being used for growing corn by the local Wampanoag Indians. The Old Pilgrim Colony used the area as a "common area" for the militia training. Town records show that this land was used by militias to practice their mustering and shooting before heading off to war.

Men from neighboring communities would come here to join rank and head north into Boston. Pending the war, military men would find themselves in immediate action or be shipped off to join established forts for war.

Frederick Olmstead Jr's father was very interested in the abolishment of slavery. He traveled through the southern states in the 1850's to collect the stories of the slaves and their owners. Olmstead published two known books in relation with his travels, "A Journey in the Seaboard Slave States" and "The Slave States."

Today, the town officials continue to recognize all the soldiers and sailors who have fought in wars to date. Every Memorial and Veterans Day celebration, local officials give orations on this site to commemorate the dedication of the military men and women.

Across the street is the Nathaniel Morton School, once a high school now an elementary school. The school got its name from Abby's brother Nathaniel who donated the land for the school.

*Look over your shoulder to see 37 Pleasant Street then, Step out to rte 3A south to continue the tour to find Sites 5 – 8.

Site 4:
The Third Congregational Society, circa 1801.
Craig/Macaferri Residence, circa 1906
37 Pleasant Street

This site occupied The Third Congregational Society. The church was built because of members wanting to separate from the First Church in Town Square. Those same members became indifferent toward the current Pastor Reverend Frederick Freeman. It was said that Rev. Freeman badgered a long time female member (Aunt Phebe Stephens) about the authority of her position having bible study with new members. Shortly after this incident the Robinson Society Church was built, revert to Site Two. This was another site for meetings for the men who came to speak to the abolitionists.

The members who disassociated themselves with this church were active abolitionists and had used this church as a meeting place. But, as fate has it they built another church that exemplifies what they believe in, The Robinson Society Church.

After awhile the entire society abandoned this church. The Rev. Frederick Freeman headed south back to Sandwich, Massachusetts where his family resided. His first wife had been ill and died in Plymouth. She is buried in Burial Hill. Having young children, shortly after the passing of this wife he remarried after his arrival in Sandwich.

This church became occupied by the Methodist Society while their church was being built in town at the top of Brewster Street now known as The Spire. The Town of Plymouth eventually gained ownership of this building and turned the structure into a high school.

The homestead which presently stands on this site was built in 1906 by a local dealer, Mr. Dexter Craig. Mr. Craig sold coal, grain and hay and later to The Macaferri family, owners of the Puritan Clothing Co., which was on downtown Main Street and remains a private residence.

Walk south along route 3A until you get to the working lights. This area is known as Wellingsley and Jabez Corner.

Site 5: The Wellingsley School House, circa 1815. Jabez Corner, behind Bradford Liquor Store

This one-room school house is tucked behind the Bradford Liquor Store, currently a storage facility. The school was named for the area which was known for at the time as Wellingsley. Originally, this school house stood across the street behind the convenient store which stand there today.

This school was the classroom for the very active junior anti-slavery children. These children would have included: the Harlow sisters, (Jane, Hannah, Ruth, Zilpha and Desire); Abigail (Abby M. Diaz) Morton, Helen Morton, Edwin Morton, and Sarah Stephens (Burton). According to a written recollection of Abby Morton, she and her young abolitionist relatives and friends tried to influence their peers on anti-slavery issues every chance they got for writing and public speaking assignments.

The young abolitionists turned to their greatest concern of freeing the nine million slaves from Africa. They raised money, attended meetings, were watchmen for adult meetings and spread the word about how wrong it was to keep brothers and sisters in bondage and be so mistreated.

Knowing how Abby Morton's father, Ichabod, was so instrumental in helping the state's first educational secretary, Mr. Mann, build the first Normal School in Bridgewater Massachusetts (k.n.a. Bridgewater State University),it won't be surprising to know how the Morton's were involved with the instruction within this one room schoolhouse as well.

Abby and Desire attended the first class at the Normal School in Bridgewater, Massachusetts nka Bridgewater State College. Sarah became a teacher and Helen became a physician in Boston.

In June of 1969, this school house was moved to its present location.

.

Site 6:
Edwin Morton's Homestead, circa 1791
218 Sandwich Street

This homestead was the childhood home of abolitionist Edwin Morton. His father, Ichabod Morton, married Susan Churchill in 1787. They had eight children: Sarah (m. L.Stephens), Ichabod (m. P. Weston first and B.Holbrook second), Hannah, Mary (Bartlett), Abigail, Betsey (m. Mr. Whiting first and Mr. Clark second), Edwin (m. B. Harlow) and Maria (m. a Churchill).

Edwin remained in this homestead with his wife (Betsey) and children Helen and Edwin. Helen removed to Boston and became a doctor; she was an abolitionist and supported the Women's Rights movement. His son Edwin stayed local, worked in the family shipping business and also supported the abolitionist movement. Abby Morton kindly refers to him numerous times as the cousin who encouraged her to write for children. Abby also described her Uncle Edwin as, "blue eyes, younger than her father, fair haired, strong for truth and progress, yet facetious withal and of quick sympathies."

Edwin and his older brother Ichabod were very close all through life. They were partners in a shipping business, I & E Morton, and were very supportive of each other's interests. These men were appointed anti-slavery agents by abolitionist leader William Lloyd Garrison. As agents they would secure local places for their meetings usually attended by abolitionists from nearby towns and great speakers.

Site 7:
Ichabod Morton's Homestead, circa 1750
212 Sandwich Street

This was the home of Abigail (Abby) Morton as a child. Abby is the youngest known abolitionist in Plymouth. The area where this house is located was known as Wellingsley or Hobshole. This homestead was a "safe/station house" as described by Abby in published interviews. It's also the site where well known literary men came to visit Ichabod to discuss the need for change and growth in various aspects of life.

Men such as Bronson Alcott, Ralph Waldo Emerson, William Lloyd Garrison and Horace Mann were friends with Ichabod Morton, (b. 1790 - d. May10, 1861), his brother Edwin and brother-in-law Lemuel Stephens. These same men organized Plymouth's first Anti-Slavery Society on the July 4, 1835, according to town historian William T. Davis. Ichabod's daughter Abby told the New England Magazine editor that she became a member of the Juvenile Anti-Slavery Society when she was eight years old in 1829.

After the early death of Abby's mother Patty Weston, her father Ichabod married Betsey Holbrook. Abby soon had five brothers: George, Nathaniel, Ichabod, Austin and Howard. Abby described her father as "tall, erect, earnest in bearing, usually of serious aspect and much given to planning for the kingdom of heaven to come on earth.

He felt he needed to free people from the cruel old orthodox ways and was an earnest worker for temperance, anti-slavery and the educational movement." In later years, family descendents began to speak about their findings in the homes from the days of slavery. The slaves would scratch (Sanskrit) their names in the wall near fireplaces or on a piece of wood to show their passing on through to Canada.

In 1851, Jonathan Walker, branded "SS" slave stealer, came to Plymouth while on his three week lecture circuit and to stir up a vigilance committee to assist runaways. While in Plymouth he and some fugitive slaves stayed in "a rough and humble cabin." Unable to find steady work after three weeks he moved on to Vermont.

President Theodore Roosevelt wrote in his autobiography, both my wife and I have the bound volumes of Our Young Folks which we preserved from our youth. I have tried to read ……… I enjoy going over Our Young Folks now nearly as much as ever. "Cast Away in the Cold," Grandfather's Struggle for a Homestead," "The William Henry Letters" (written by Abigail Morton Diaz) and a dozen other like them were first –class, good healthy stories, interesting in the first place , and in the next place teaching manliness, decency, and good conduct. …..

Site 8:
The Stephen's Homestead, circa 1854
Stephen's Lane (on the shore)

    This was the site of the home of abolitionist Lemuel Stephens who married Sarah (Aunt Sally) Morton. They had two children: Sarah (m. C. Burton) and Lemuel, (m.Ann Buckminster). Lemuel Stephens was a shipping business partner and brother-in-law to Ichabod. Morton. The Stephens family had two known homesteads on their estate, now known as Stephen's Lane.
    Today, only one homestead remains which is found down by the shoreline south side (a private residence) at the end of Stephens Lane. The home on the north side of the Stephens Lane was across the street from the house pictured on book cover was demolished for current condominiums. William Stephens and his wife Esther Allen lived here until his death in 1851. Esther died in 1837. They had two children, a daughter Phebe m. Capt.T.J.Cotton, who resided in the family home after the death of her husband. She was 54 years old and passed away on the 5th of July 1844. Their son Lemuel b.1814 married Sarah Morton, known as Aunt Sally.
    This entire family were dedicated abolitionists. Daughter Sarah, like her mother Sarah (Aunt Sally), and Aunt Phebe Cotton, were part of the women's abolitionist society. The young Sarah married her brother's best friend Charles Burton. She became a much admired teacher in Plymouth. Charles also taught in Plymouth and later became the town's superintendent of schools. Sarah's obituary (enclosed)

reveals the dedication of her family's involvement true to abolitionism, education and women's rights.

Lemuel's sister Phebe,(Aunt Phebe), married young to Capt. Thomas Cotton on the 13th of March 1810 in Rhode Island witnessed by Alpheus and Sarah Amedown. On the 9th of June, 1819 Thomas died in action while in Havana, Cuba. Phebe never remarried and lived her life out in her parents' homestead.

Her husband is buried in Burial Hill in his family plot #480 near the powder house. She is buried in her family plot in Oak Grove Cemetery, Due to strict pastoral rules, which was related to her excommunication of the First Church, it appears she lost the ability to be buried with her husband.

Through Abby's stories, Aunt Phebe was an active abolitionist for the Anti-Slavery Society and very dedicated to her religion, conducting bible studies at her parents' home. Today, portraits of Lemuel and Sarah Morton-Stephens are owned by the Plymouth Antiquarian Society, seen in the Hedge House Museum.

Abby Morton Diaz describes her Aunt Sally in one of her period interviews as: "One of Plymouth's dedicated laborers and helped provide visiting lecturers." Aunt Sally was "small in stature, all animation, a brisk worker impatient with idlers, quick to plan and accomplish!" Abby's Uncle Lemuel Stephens was "slower in movement, more deliberate in thought and speech, likely to be discussing creeds or politics, a man of fine mind and his well thought conclusions were sure to be excellently worded." Abby thought highly of her reformist relatives. "They were a united couple, thinkers, keen sighted for principle and advocates of justice and freedom."

Ichabod Morton – (Abigail's father)
Photo: Courtesy of The Plymouth Antiquarian Society

The Morton Family Tree
Abigail Morton Diaz (Nov. 22, 1821-March 31, 1904)
This shows how Abigail descends from George and Julian Morton. The Mortons arrived in Plimoth on the ship Anne in 1623. As Oceanus was born on the Mayflower in passage to the New World, so did Abigail's 6th great grandfather Ephraim in 1623.

George m. Julian Carpenter (sister to Gov. Bradford's second wife)
Children: 1613 Nathaniel, 1615 Patience, 1616 John, 1618 Sarah, 1623 * Ephraim (Patience was the mother of Elder Thomas Faunce, who gave the story of the Plymouth Rock.)

Ephraim m. Ann Cooper in 1644
Children: 1645 George, 1748 * Ephraim, 1651 Rebecca, 1653 Josiah, 1667 Thomas. Patience m. 2nd Mary (Shelley) Harlow (widow of William Harlow, 3rd wife)
Children: none (Mary had five daughters with William)

Ephraim m. Hannah
Children: 1667 Hannah (m. B. Warren), 1678 * Ephraim, 1680 John, 1683 Joseph, 1685 Ebenezer.

Ephraim m. Susanna Morton
Children: 1713 Susanna, 1715 Hannah, 1718 Sarah (m. Warren), 1722 * Ephraim, 1724 Abigail (m. Morton), 1730 Ichabod.

Ephraim m. Sarah (?)
1747 Ephraim, 1751 Osborn, 1753 Edward, 1756 * Ichabod, Rebecca (m. 1784 Daniel Jackson)

Ichabod m. Zilpha Thayer
Children: Ephraim. *Ichabod, Hannah (Clark), Polly (Whiting), Zilpha (Bartlett), Susan (Sears)

Ichabod m. Susan Churchill in 1787
Children: Sarah (m. L. Stephens), * 1790 Ichabod, Hannah, Mary (Bartlett), Abigail, Betsey (m. 1st Whiting and 2nd Clark), Edwin (m. Betsey T. Harlow) and Maria (m. Churchill)

Ichabod m. Patty Weston in 1818
Children: * Abigail 1821
Ichabod m. 2nd Betsey Holbrook
Children: 1829 George E., 1831 Nathaniel, 1833 Ichabod, 1834 Austin, 1836 Howard

Abigail Morton m. Manuel Diaz of Havana, Cuba (1845)
  Children: 1847 Roberto, 1849 Manuel

Andrea M. Daly

Old Colony Memorial Newspaper Ad July 4th 1847

Anti-Slavery convention in Baptist Church. Addresses by Messers, Douglass, Buffam, Remond, and Moody, Resolutions presenting by Loring Moody and Parker Pillsbury.

Old Colony Memorial Newspaper Ad 1850

Dec.21 and 22, 1850, Old Colony Anti-Slavery Society celebrate In the lower part of the High School building at the Green. Addresses by Geo. Thompson, Esq., M. P. William Lloyd Garrison, Wendell Phillips, and Frederick Douglas. Chas. P. Morse

Site 9:
The First Baptist Church, circa 1822-61. Spring Lane, Plymouth

Spring lane is now a tarred road to the left of the Governor Carver Hotel. There is an arch at the entrance which leads to where this old road was once. The road now leads into the Burial Hill Cemetery. Walk to the top of the road and this was the site of The First Baptist Church. Unfortunately, this one room church was razed years ago due to a fire. The Baptist Society has built a few churches in town – top of Leyden, top of Cole's Hill – until they permanently settled on Westerly Road in town. You can see this First Baptist Church and learn more about the history of Plymouth's Baptist Churches by visiting their web site: **www.fbcplymouth.cjb.net.**

The abolitionists used the First Baptist Church for their conventions. In April of 1847, the Old Colony Memorial local newspaper noted the guests for one such convention. Guests were noted as being Mssrs: Douglas, Buffum, Remond, Moody, Parker and Pillsbury. These men (with the exception of Mr. Buffum) were speakers for the lecture circuit for the anti-slavery movement. Every meeting or convention for the men's Old Colony Anti-Slavery Society would have speakers noted in an ad placed in the local newspaper
. Mr. Frederick Douglas, slave and abolitionist along with his long time travel companion Mr. Buffum, Mr. Remond is also known as Charles Lenox Remond who was born to a black free couple in Salem, Massachusetts and was very involved in the lecture circuit to speak against slavery. He and his sister Sarah Parker Remond spent their lives lecturing to abolish black slavery. They had seven siblings and their parents moved the family from Salem because of the town pressure of not being able to school their children in public schools. Msser Moody, Rev. Granville Moody of Ohio. Messer. Parker Pillsbury. Pillsbury, (m. Sarah Sargent), was another minister and eloquent speaker and a friend to all the anti-slavery members of Plymouth.

Site 10:
The Sherman Building, circa 1887
Main Street, Plymouth Center

This downtown building is recognized by the **embossment of 1887** still seen at the top of the building. This year represents the year which this building underwent renovations, not when it was originally built. The building was known as the Sherman & Barnes building. See the newspaper article below which was found in the local paper, the Old Colony Memorial, 1887.

As mentioned a number of times in my book, this building was important to the Juvenile and Women's Anti-Slavery Society. These members were allowed to have a Reading Room on the second floor of this building, which was a great responsibility for young girls between the ages of eight and 15. This Reading Room held all the anti-slavery literature the members collected from attending various anti-slavery meetings or events.

The Juvenile Society managed to get the *Liberator* newspaper founded by William Lloyd Garrison for their Reading Room thanks to adult relatives who had business in Boston and would return with this newspaper for all to read.

Abby Morton talked about this Reading Room during interviews with period magazines. She and her cousins, along with the Harlow sisters, were very active supporting the Reading Room and raising money for their belief in the anti-slavery movement. Young women found their future husbands within the anti-slavery societies. Hannah Harlow was one of the older members. Her future husband (George Adams) not only believed in the anti-slavery movement, conveniently worked in the hat store which was below the Reading Room.

.In order to raise money to help free the nine million black slaves, they would make and sell candy and ice cream in the Reading Room. They also would collect pennies by giving up their favorite food each week and going from house to house to see if they could convince anyone else to give their pennies for this very heartfelt cause. According to Abby Morton, the anti-slavery movement was not popular in town.

When the girls went to collect pennies from various townspeople they were confronted with a lot of ridicule, called "nigger lovers" and were told that they didn't know what they were doing. The young women were very strong in their belief because their entire family was usually involved with supporting the anti-slavery movement. The youngest women helped the adults by being "watchmen"; while their meetings were held. They would signal when unwanted mobs showed up. The Reading Room had a sign outside the building which got great recognition one night, "it was besmeared with tar", after the signing of the Fugitive Slave Law in 1850. It was this action that made the girls feel their work was being recognized.

Site 11:
North Street, Plymouth Center

North Street is the second oldest street in Plymouth, the first being Leyden Street.

9-14 North Street

This was the homestead of the Weston family. The building housed three Weston families and was known as the Weston Block. Abby Morton's mother was born in #14, her grandmother, known as "Ma'am Weston," had a nursery school, known as a "Dame School" which was attended by most of the children who lived on North Street. The school is fondly remembered by student Laura Russell in her book, "Laura Russell Remembers." Abby's grandfather was a seafaring man and died off the coast of Nantucket when Abby's mother was quite young. In Abby's later years after marriage, she returned to Plymouth and taught dance school in 9 North Street. The story that surrounds this building is that the family wanted to be able to visit each other during the winter without having to go outside, so they built their homes so a door would open into each other's home.

#26 North Street

The Jackson-Russell-Whitfield House circa 1738. Today, this house is a bed and breakfast owned by Dr. Whitfield. This house had additions added on seen in the back of the home. Dr.Whitfield also enjoys playing musical instruments and has performances opened to the public.

Samuel Jackson built the house, His daughter Mary married John Russell, hence the onset of the Russell families ownership. All men were very involved with traveling the seas, the whaling business, ship building and in trade abroad. After retiring from their voyages, they got involved with town affairs.

Deborah Spooner was sister to Bourne Spooner, children of Capt. Nathaniel and Mary (Holmes) Spooner. Deborah married a John Russell. Her husband John was known as "Deep Water John" because of his travels abroad. The Russell men also supported Bourne Spooners' Cordage Company venture. Deborah and John had five children, their youngest daughter was Laura Russell. Laura was a local writer who stationed herself on Nantucket Island during the time when abolitionist Frederick Douglass spoke for an anti-slavery convention. Laura wrote about her life in and around Plymouth, her book is called, "Laura Russell Remembers".

27 North Street

The Spooner House Museum circa 1749. This house had five generations of the Spooner family living here. The original furniture of this family remains in the house as well as their letters from the 19th century. Mary Spooner, sister to Bourne Spooner, married her cousin Ephraim Spooner and resided in this house. Her husband and his brother James ran a store that was on the corner of Leyden and Main Street. Ephraim was appointed Plymouth's Postmaster in 1840.He was also known as a leader in Plymouth's Temperance Society established in 1825.

Many letters kept by the family are owned by the Antiquarian Society. Letters that I was able to read were in relation to Mary's travels with brother Bourne and or just with his wife Hannah. Letter writing was Mary's way of keeping in touch with her daughter Esther and husband. Esther was very detailed in her letters about what was going on at home and in Plymouth. Esther was very supportive of her mother's travels.

In the attic there is a latch that slides down on the door from inside the attic. The attic is very spacious and was designed to have occupants. The Spooners had a couple of female servants for Mrs. Frona Spooner. One Spooner servant came from Ireland, her daughter Evelyn Reardon lived in Plymouth and a friend of my grandmother. Evelyn's home at 19 Billington Street was recognized by local historian Reverend Peter Gomes as the earliest African American Church in Plymouth. It was a private residence when Evelyn resided there and remains one today. The AME church today is located in town on Sever Street. There are guided tours of this Spooner home during the summer. The docents tell the story of the five generations of Spooner's who lived here.

35 North Street

This house, circa 1829, was owned by abolitionists Zilpha Harlow Spooner and Nathaniel Bourne Spooner. The couple married in Nahant on June 14, 1851 and shortly after bought their first home at auction for $300.

Zilpha began in the anti-slavery movement as a juvenile. She was a daughter of abolitionist Ephraim Harlow. Nathaniel was the son of abolitionist Bourne and Hannah Spooner. In reading this tour, you will have read how their families were well known participants in abolishing slavery. Zilpha and Nathaniel had two children, Wendall and Ruth. Ruth was the last survivor, neither child married.

Zilpha published a small book of her favorite poems, "Poems of Pilgrims." After slavery was abolished, Zilpha focused her energy on the Women's Suffrage Movement as did her friends.

Today this residence has one owner and is used for a private residence and a business.

Site 12:
The Mayflower Society House, circa 1756
3 Winslow Street

This was the home of Ralph Waldo Emerson's second wife, Lydian Jackson. They were married in the front east room. Ralph and Lydian were known abolitionists from documents preserved in Concord, Massachusetts where they resided as a married couple.

Plymouth is where the couple met. Mr. Emerson made a number of appearances in Plymouth giving a speech about his writings. Lydian grew up amongst many women who were very involved with the betterment for the lives and of all individuals. Lydian and her friends would have showed up for all visitors who would come into their small town to talk about what was going on in the country.

Mrs. Emerson was a member of Concord's Women's Anti-Slavery Society. Ralph was very busy in the lecture circuits for various causes. This home was built by Edward Winslow, grandson to the Pilgrim Edward Winslow. Lydian's father, Charles Jackson, bought this house when in business with his five other brothers. Charles was a selectman in town. He and his brothers were involved with whaling, fishing in the Grand Banks, ship building and foreign trade. Numerous architectural renovations have been made to this house since its first ownership. Currently, this house is owned by descendants of The Mayflower Society and is opened to the public with guided tours during the summer season.

Site 13:
The Old Colony Club House
25 Court Street, Plymouth Center

Charles G. Davis (May 30, 1820-1903) was an active abolitionist. In 1851, he assisted in the rescue of the fugitive slave "Shadrach" Minkins in Boston, Massachusetts. Shadrach was the first fugitive slave to be arrested in New England under the Fugitive Slave Law of 1850. Mr. Davis was dedicated to the anti-slavery cause regardless of his political ties. Mr. Davis' involvement can be further understood in the book "Shadrach Minkins" by Gary Collison, published through the Harvard University Press in 1998.

There were many Davis men born in town who loved this town, they embraced its history. Their interest in Plymouth was deep. They dedicated themselves to the improvement of Plymouth architecturally, politically and educationally. A number of the Davis men went to Harvard College and traveled extensively.

This building now occupies the Old Colony Club which was a residence of Mr. Davis. This is the oldest men's club in the country. They celebrate the landing of the Pilgrims with a 5am morning walk on the 21st of December to Coles Hill. Tradition was to shoot a cannon at the top of Coles Hill. Upon their return to clubhouse they sat down to a traditional feast of Sauquetach, dishes of clams, oysters, cod, venison, sea fowl, eel and baked Indian whortle berry pudding.

Edward Winslow Watson

Site 14:
Clark's Island, Plymouth Bay

Edward Winslow Watson, "Lord of the Isle," nicknamed by Daniel Webster, owned and lived out on Clark's Island in Plymouth Bay. Edward enjoyed hosting various types of people; authors, poets, political, temperance, reformers, naturalists, etc. Summers out on the island gave many a chance to educate their mind and extend their friendship. Mary Grew and Margaret Burleigh, abolitionist from Pennsylvania, visited Edward Watson in the summer of 1865. In Mary's diary she spoke of Edward as "a rare character, worth knowing, who welcomes and appreciates true reformers, and persons who do their own thinking". One of our earlier local historians, William T. Russell published a eulogy for Edward Winslow Watson. Buried on Clark's Island, never married and was known to many as a man with many talents. The Watson family owns homes on the island but the town of Plymouth now owns the island. Clark's Island can best be seen up on Burial Hill above Town Square.

Edward wrote "Verses" which he published in 1877, A Parting Gift to his Friends. His last lines written days before his death were:"From Standish Hill the Island Bay, The distant view of Salt house Beach, The opening landscape far away, Beyond the eyesights utmost reach………

Mary Grew   Sally Holley

Site 15:
The Lyle Family Homestead, circa early18thc.
174 Court Street, Plymouth\

This home was first occupied by Pastor Nathaniel Leonard, He was a graduate of Harvard, Pastor of The First Church in Town until he resigned in 1775 due to his poor health. The local newspaper in 1984, Maggie Mills "Then and Now" editorials first revealed the site of a cobble stone archway within the home which lead to a tunnel now bricked up. Town stories revealed a tunnel lead to the home in the rear of the property near the hill, its purpose is still speculative.

Mr. George Lyle bought the home for $900. Dollars, In 1870. He and his wife (Jerry Randall) and two sons lived in the home until the end of their lives. George was a free slave from the south. The sons James and Richard were bachelors and both lived into their eighties. James passed away in 1971and Richard in1965. The sons were well known by my cousin Norma Perron.

Norma stated Richard (Dick) would visit her Uncle Bill Pioppi's restaurant in town, where the All American Diner stands today. Dick stood tall and thin, he loved to joke and talked with Norma's mother Ann and the other kitchen workers. When Ann had a stroke, he walked from his home to their home near the Training Green to check on her and help out with her dinner. Norma's father had passed away earlier and while she was still in high school Mr. Lyle's help was so appreciated and was a true friend.

The only known and documented tunnel made to rescue fugitive slaves is in Boston at The Francis Jackson's homestead. The homestead is a museum and open to the public.

Northern homesteads from Plymouth were known to be part of "The Liberty Line" for fugitive slaves. Northern men and women who dared to gamble their lives for slaves had to have a tight network or pay the consequences in court. There was always financial or political assistance through the vigilance committees but, if money or messages got into the wrong hands their help was useless. Plymouth was off the path for the "known" Liberty Line but found ways to help the cause.

Site 16:
Bourne Spooner's Homestead, circa 1824
373 Court Street, Plymouth

Mr. Bourne Spooner (Feb. 2, 1790-July 1870) married Hannah (Bartlett) in 1813. Husband and wife became known abolitionists in Plymouth. Many family members of Bourne Spooner were abolitionists and showed their support either as laborers or politically. Records were not kept well for any northern abolition society so details had to be found elsewhere. The local newspaper, the Old Colony Memorial, advertised anti-slavery meetings signed by Bourne Spooner, President of the Anti-Slavery Society. This gave proof of their existence as well as autobiographies by other lecturing abolitionists who came to Plymouth.

Abby Morton was interviewed by the New England Magazine and spoke of her memories of the anti-slavery meetings in and away from Plymouth. Lecturer Lydia Maria Child and Mr. Edward Quincy, among others including fugitive slaves, came to Plymouth for the stories of slavery. They were involved in the lecture circuit which was organized by the agents in each town.

Bourne founded the Cordage Company in 1824, which his house fronted. He paid $800 for his home which has had renovations. Bourne visited a number of businesses in the south before co-founding his own. He had developed a self-sufficient community for all the workers who came from abroad, (Germans, Italians, Irish, and Portuguese), to work for the Cordage. Today his home is the Davis Funeral Home. The Cordage Company was very prosperous without the use of slaves and didn't close their doors until 1969.

The Anti-Slavery Alphabet

This alphabet was printed for The Anti-Slavery Fair in Philadelphia in 1847:

A is for an Abolitionist – A man who wants to free the wretched slave – and give all an equal liberty.

B is a Brother with a skin of somewhat darker hue, But in our Heavenly Father's sight, he is a dear as you.

C is the Cotton field. In which this injured brother's driven. When, as the white man's slave, he tells from early morn till even.

D is the Driver, cold and stern, who follows, whip in hand, to punish those who dare to rest, or disobey command.

E is the Eagle soaring high; an emblem of the free: But while we chain our brother man – our type he cannot be.

F is the heart sick fugitive, the slave who runs away, and travels through the dreary night, But hides himself by day.

G is the Gong, whose rolling around, before the morning light, calls up the little sleeping slave to labor until night.

H is the Hound his master trained, and called to scent the track of the unhappy fugitive, and bring him trembling back.

I is the Infant, from the arms of his fond mother torn, and at a public auction, sold with horses, cows, and corn.

J is the Jail, upon whose floor that wretched mother lay, until her cruel master came and carried her away.

K is the Kidnapper, who stole that little child and mother – shrieking, it clung around her, but he tore them from each other.

L is the Lash that brutally he swung around his head, threatening that "if it cried again, he'd whip it till 'twas dead.

M is the Merchant of the north, who buys what slaves produce – so they are stolen, whipped and worked, for his, and for our use.

N is the Negro, rambling free in his far distant home, delighting 'neath the palm trees' shade and cocoa-nut to roam.

O is the Orange tree, that bloomed beside his cabin door, when white men stole him from his home to see it never more.

P is the Parent, sorrowing, and weeping all alone – the child he loved to lean upon, his only son, is gone!

Q is the Quarter, where the slave on coarsest food is fed, and where, with toil and sorrow worn, he seeks his wretched bed.

R is the "Rice-swamp, dank and lone," where weary, day by day, he labors till the fever wastes his strength and life away.

S is the Sugar that the slave is toiling hard to make, to put into your pie and tea, your candy, and your cake.

T is the Tobacco plant, Raised by slave labor too; a poisonous and nasty thing, for gentleman to chew.

U is for Upper Canada, Where the poor slave has found rest after all his wanderings, for it is British ground!

V is the Vessel, in whose dark, noisome, and stifling hold, hundreds of Africans are packed, brought o'er the seas, and sold.

W is the Whipping post, to which the slave is bound, while on his naked back, the lash makes many a bleeding wound.

X is for Xerses, famed of yore; a warrior stern was he. He fought with swords; let truth and love our only weapon be.

Y is for Youth – the time for all. Bravely to war with sin; and think not it can ever be too early to begin.

Z is a Zealous man, sincere, faithful and just, and true: An earnest pleader for the slave – will you not be so too?

Original microfiche came from Oberlin College Library, E449; LCP 19, 652

Copy found at The Thomas Crane Public Library, Quincy, MA, ILL#269836

Suggested Reading

Brown, Francis F. The Everyday Life of Abraham Lincoln.

Brown, Ira V. Mary Grew (Abolitionist and Feminist-1813-1896), Associated University Presses, Inc., 1991.

Channing, Marion L., Laura Russell Remembers, An Old Plymouth Manuscript with notes by Marion L. Channing. Reynolds-DeWalt Printing,
Inc., New Bedford, Massachusetts, 1970.

Child, Lydia Maria. Isaac T. Hopper: A True Life, Boston, Massachusetts,
John P. Jewett & Co. 1853.

Clarke, James Freeman. Anti-Slavery Days, New York, United States Book Co., 1883.

Collinson, Gary. Shadrach Minkins: From Fugitive Slave to Citizen .Cambridge, Massachusetts; Harvard University Press, 1998.

Cooke, George Willis. Early Letters of George Wm. Curtis to John S.Dwight. Harper & Brothers Publishers, New York and London, 1898.

Curtis, Edith Roelker. A Season In Utopia. New York, Thomas Nelson &Sons, 1961.

Davis, William T. Plymouth Memories of an Octogenarian, Plymouth, Massachusetts, The Memorial Press; by the Bittinger Bros., 1906.

Davis, William T. Ancient Landmarks of Plymouth, Boston, Massachusetts; A. William and Company, 1883.

Drew, Benjamin. The Refugee: or the Narratives of Fugitive Slaves in Canada. Cleveland, Ohio; John P. Jewett and Co., 1856.

Drew, Benjamin. Refugee: A North Side View of Slavery. Reading,
Massachusetts; Addison-Wesley Publishing Company; 1969.

Elliot, Charles W. The Harvard Classics; Emperor Marcus Aurelius. New York, P.F. Collier & Son Corp., 62nd printing, 1969.

Holley, Sallie. A Life For Liberty – Anti-Slavery And Other Letters. New York, Negro University Press, 1969. Pg.86-90.

Sernett, Milton C. Abolition's Axe. Syracuse University Press, Syracuse, New York, 1984.

*Samuel May, George B. Emerson, and Thomas J. Mumford., Life of Samuel Joseph May. Boston, Massachusetts; Roberts Brothers. 1873.

May, Samuel J. An Address To the Normal Association, Bridgewater, Massachusetts, August 8, 1855.

May, Samuel J. Some Recollections of our Antislavery Conflict. Boston, Massachusetts; Fields, Osgood, & Co. 1869.

Morgan, James. Abraham Lincoln – The Boy And The Man. New York, Grosset & Dunlap Publishers, 1912.

Olmstead, Frederick Law. The Slave States before the Civil War. Revised and enlarged 14th edition. New York; Capricorn Books, 1959.

Parker, Theodore. The Trial of Theodore Parker, for the Misdemeanor of 33 A Speech in Faneuil Hall against Kidnapping. pg.134-149. New York; Negro University Press, reprinted 1970.

Roosevelt, Theodore. An Autobiography. The MacMillan Company, New York, 1913, pg.20

Sernett, Milton C. Abolition's Axe. Syracuse, New York; Syracuse University Press, 1986.

Stern, Madeleine B. We The Women – Career Firsts of Nineteenth Century America. University of Nebraska Press, 1994.

Thacher, James. History of Plymouth, Massachusetts: From its First Settlement in 1620 To The Present Time (1835). Salem, Massachusetts. Higginson Book Co., Reprint 1991.

* The Plymouth Cordage Company Proceedings At Its 75th Anniversary: 1824-1899. Inside Photo: Bourne Spooner

Richardson, Joe M. Trial and Imprisonment of Jonathan Walker, at
Pensacola, Florida. Gainesville, Florida; the University Presses of Florida, 1974

Quick, Robert Herbert. Essays on Educational Reformers. D. Appleton and Company, New York, 1897.

Thoreau, Henry David (1817-1862), "Slavery in Massachusetts."

Books by Abigail Morton Diaz

Year Title Co-Authors
1861 Pink and Blue
1861 Liberating the Home
1869 King Bronde
1870 The William Henry Letters
1871 William Henry and his friends
1875 The SchoolMaster's Trunk
1876 Neighborhood talks
1876 A story-book for the children
1877 Jimmyjohns: and other stories
1877 Prang's Natural History Series for Children Calkins, N.A.
1878 Cat Family Calkins, N.A.
1878 Cow Family Calkins, N.A.
1878 Scratching Birds Calkins, N.A.
1878 Wading Birds Calkins, N.A.
1880 Brave little goose-girl; little stories ...
1880 Christmas morning; little stories for little...
1880 Mercy Jane: little stories ...
1880 Molasses candy; little stories...
1880 Merry Christmas: little stories...
1881 Domestic Problems: work and culture in Tweenit...
1881 King Grimalkum and Pussyanita,
1881 Lucy Maria
1882 Chronicles of the Stimpcett family: and
1882 Fireside Chronicles of the family ...
1883 The Cats' Arabian Nights
1887 By Bury to Beacon Street
1887 Leaves of Healing
1887 The Religious Training of Children
1888 Jamie and Joe
1889 In the Strength of the Lord
1889 Conventions during the Anti-Slavery Agitation
1891 Mother Goose's Christmas Party

1893 Only a Flock of Women
1895 The Law of Perfection
1901 The Flatiron and the Red Cloak
1906 Those People from Skyton...
1909 Polly Cologne
1915 The New Life Training of Children

Time Line During the Life of Abigail Morton Diaz

1783 Slavery comes to an end in Massachusetts; Chief Justice William Cushing concluded that the idea of slavery is inconsistent with the state's constitution.
1810 March 13, Phebe Stephens m. Thomas Jackson Cotton in R.I.
1818 Phebe Cotton (Abby's cousin) is baptized as the adult wife of T.J.C. Nov. 15, Ichabod Morton m. Patty Weston of Plymouth
1819 June 9, Capt. Thomas J. Cotton dies in Havana, buried in Burial Hill (34 years old)
1820 Plymouth's population was approximately 4,384 (today's pop. is approx. 56,000); Plymouth's second Court House was built in Court Square; statesman DanielWebster gave Opening Address; 200th Anniversary of the Landing of the Pilgrims
1821 Nov. 22, Abigail Morton was born to Ichabod and Patty (Weston) Morton
1822 The Old Colony Memorial newspaper established; reformer & author Caroline Wells Healey Dall was born, 1822-1912; slave revolt in South Carolina, 35 slaves are hung
1823 Abby becomes a member of the Fragment Society in the Town of Plymouth on April 16; Phebe Cotton and Ichabod Morton request to be dismissed from the First Church. (She wanted to connect herself with the Third Church of Plymouth on Pleasant Street overlooking the Training Green. Ichabod had not stated his church.)
1824 The Cordage Company is founded in North Plymouth by Bourne Spooner
1827 Patty Weston Morton dies (b. Dec.23 1791-d. Aug. 2), Abby Morton's mother
1828 Ichabod Morton m. 2nd Betsey Holbrook.
1829 Jan. 1, Ichabod buys "Hobshole" from Mrs. Jackson; Feb. 26, Hannah Harlow m.George Adams in Plymouth; Dec. 13, Abby's first brother is born, George Morton.
1830 Jan. 20, Jane Harlow m. Atwood L. Drew, Plymouth (Abolitionist); Helen Hunt Jackson is born, 1830-1885, author, Transcendentalist; Black Abolitionist David Walker dies in Boston; William Lloyd Garrison kept his spirit alive
1831 Robinson Congregational Church built near entrance of Pleasant Street, Plymouth; backyard of Ephraim Harlow.

May 20, Nathaniel Morton is born (Abby's second brother); Jan. 1, The Liberator
Newspaper is started by W.L. Garrison; Nat Turner slave revolt in Virginia
1832 New England Anti-Slavery Society is founded by W.L. Garrison; May 18, Jerusha T. Harlow m. Samuel Talbot (Ephraim's daughter); Dec. 23, Edwin Morton is born to Edwin and Betsey Morton (Abby's cousin who inspired her to write her stories)
1833 Scarlet fever hits Plymouth (167 deaths); Abolitionists of Plymouth began following W.L. Garrison; The Liberator, an Anti-Slavery newspaper edited by W. L. Garrison, is brought home by Uncle Edwin Morton; Abby joins the Jr. Anti-Slavery Society in Plymouth, she was voted Secretary; Feb. 7, Ichabod Morton III is born (Abby's third brother); American Anti-Slavery Society is founded, W.L. Garrison was its President for 22 terms; April 8, Mercy Bisbee m. Daniel Jackson of Plymouth (North Street residents), Daniel's mother was a Morton, Mercy became a Homeopathic Doctor
1834 Dec. 16, Austin Morton is born (Abby's fourth brother); Town Selectmen give North Street its permanent name (previously named Queen, Howland and New Street – it's the second oldest street in Plymouth); W.L. Garrison marries Eliza Benson, they have seven children; November, Kingston, Mass., Anti-Slavery Society formed
1835 May, Honorable James G. Birney, of Kentucky and later Alabama, lectured at the Annual Massachusetts Antislavery Society in Boston; July 4, The Anti-Slavery Meeting was held in Robinson Society Church in Plymouth; Ralph Waldo Emerson lectures in town invited by Rev. Kendall, Mr. Emerson met his second wife in Plymouth, Lydian Jackson of North Street; George Thompson, a fiery England abolitionist was driven out of the U.S.; May 28, Capt. Jacob Covington dies (m.Patty Holbrook, sister to Betsey Morton, second wife to Abby's father, Ichabod Morton); Sept. 14, Lydian Jackson marries Ralph Waldo Emerson in Plymouth; Oct.21, W.L. Garrison seized on Washington Street in Boston by a mob, they coiled a rope around his neck but unsuccessfully carried out their intent
1836 Oct. 24, Howard Morton is born (Abby's fifth brother)
1837 Financial panic hits the area; November, Elijah P. Lovejoy, an abolitionist editor, killed for defending his press
1840 Abby attends the Bridgewater Normal School, first class for women teachers; May, Local abolitionists attend World's Anti-Slavery Convention in London, England, but the women were denied seats on the convention floor
1841 Abby graduates from The First Class of The Bridgewater Normal School (see classlist); Frederick Douglass speaks at Anti Slavery Convention on

Nantucket (from this point, Douglass was encouraged to be a lecturing agent for the Massachusetts Anti-Slavery Society)
1842 Abby lives at Brook Farm in W. Roxbury Mass., she teaches "The Infant Class";Abby meets Manuel Diaz at Brook Farm; little Waldo, son of Lydian and Ralph W.Emerson, dies of scarlet fever; furor over failure to release fugitive slave George Latimer unites abolitionists; Quaker Isaac T. Hopper speaks at the Anti-Slavery Fair in Boston
1843 Bunker Hill Monument dedicated, Daniel Webster gave oration; Massachusetts Law Prohibiting Interracial Marriage ends (est. 1786); July 21, Ruth Harlow dies, an abolitionist and friend of Abby Morton Diaz; Isaac T. Hopper returns to Boston, he speaks in the Armory Hall for the Anti-Slavery Fair; Anti-Slavery Meeting in Waltham, Mass., attended by Horace Mann and Samuel May
1844 July 5, Phebe Stephens Cotton dies of consumption, consort to Thomas Jackson Cotton, Abby's Aunt Phebe (due to Phebe excommunicating herself from The First Church, she was not allowed to be buried with her husband on Burial Hill – she is buried in Plymouth's Oak Grove Cemetery); Aug. 1, Lydian (Jackson) Emerson attends the Women's Anti-Slavery Society Meeting in Concord, Mass.; April 3, Plymouth Colony's Anti-Slavery Society advertises its next meeting; Dec. 7, ad in the OCM on Capt. J. Walker, branded with "SS" on right hand for stealing slaves in Pensacola, Fla.; Dec. 11, Old Colony Memorial advertises Leyden Hall Lectures, "The influence of Commerce upon personal Freedom," by W. Phillips.; Dec. 21, ad in local newspaper, "Anti-Slavery Lectures," Theodore Parker speaks in the Town Hall in Town Square
1845 July 27, Jonathan Walker arrives in Massachusetts to give his first lecture in Lynn, he held up his famous branded hand; Maria Weston Chapman wrote the introduction to Mr. Walker's book "Trial And Imprisonment"; Oct. 6, Abigail Morton marries Manuel Diaz of Havana, Cuba
1846 Old Colony Rail Road Company is established in Plymouth; Jonathan Walker published "A brief view of American Chattelized Humanity and Its Supports" and "A Picture of Slavery for Youth"
1847 June 4, first son, Roberto Diaz, born in Plymouth to Abby and Manuel Diaz; Anti- Slavery Fair in Philadelphia, Pa.; Anti-Slavery Alphabet is originated; Frederick Douglass publishes The North Star newspaper geared toward blacks; William Wells Brown comes to Massachusetts and speaks on the Anti-Slavery circuit. (He is the author of Clotted, President Jefferson's black daughter)
1848 June 24, Desire Harlow dies of typhus fever, abolitionist and teacher, she was a watch guard for the Anti-Slavery Meetings in Plymouth during her

adolescent years; William and Ellen Craft escaped from a plantation in Macon, Ga., owned by Robert Collins, and go on the abolitionist lecture circuit with William Wells Brown

1849 July 4, The Anti-Slavery Convention was held in Pleasure Island Grove, Abington, Mass. (see the anti-slavery song); Aug. 31, second son Manuel Diaz born in Plymouth to Manuel and Abby Diaz; Harriet Tubman escapes slavery and returns to help others escape

1850 Federal Fugitive Slave Act allowed white bounty hunters to legally chase down slaves in northern states, many Bostonian fugitives, including William and Ellen Craft and Shadrach Minkins, were harassed and needed assistance from TheVigilance Committees to dodge southern agents; Manuel Diaz builds a home in the Wellingsley area of Plymouth, east of Abby's father's homestead on Sandwich Street; February, Parker Pillsbury spoke in Tyler Cobb's Hall in North Bridgewater regarding slavery as a sin (History of Plymouth . . . Vol. I pg. 65); Margaret Fuller dies, b.1810, Transcendentalist, poet, philosopher and critic, "The nation was deaf in regard to the evils of slavery; and those who have to speak to deaf people naturally acquire the habit of saying everything on a very high key"; Sept. 18, President Millard Fillmore signed Fugitive Slave Law, creating panic for Southern fugitive slaves and free black men in the North; October, Theodore Parker visits Plymouth (Chapter 11 "Fugitive Slaves: Trumpets and Alarums"), he returns home to find out the Crafts were being hunted by the slave-hunters; October, Jerry McHenry arrested as a slave in Syracuse, N.Y., his story became known as "The Rescue of Jerry"; Oct. 14, Boston Vigilance Committee was formed

1851 Abby publishes her first book "Liberating the Home"; Sojourner Truth gives her first speech in Akron, Ohio, "Ain't I a Woman?"; Feb. 18, Frederic Wilkins, a fugitive slave from Virginia, known as "Shadrach" was seized while in Boston working at The Cornhill Coffee House; April 3, Thomas Sims, a fugitive slave, was seized in Boston by Southern agents; June 14, Zilpha Washburn Harlow marries Nathaniel Bourne Spooner in Nahant, Mass.; June 12, Plymouth County Anti- Slavery Society gives a farewell soiree to George Thompson. Esq. M.P., Bourne Spooner, President; May, Jonathan Walker began the first Vigilance Committee inPlymouth; William Stephens Sr. died

1852 Aug. 22, An Anti-Slavery Meeting at Bourne Spooner's home in North Plymouth, attended by Miss Sallie Holley (b. Feb. 27, 1818-Jan. 12, 1893), an abolitionist lecturer from Pennsylvania; December, Mr. and Mrs. (Angelina Grimke) Theodore Weld in New Jersey, known abolitionists; October, Mott Mansion in Pennsylvania accommodates abolitionist lecturers while they are in the area to speak

Self Guided Tour: Abolitionists of Plymouth

1853 Jan. 9, Sallie Holley visits Weston family in Weymouth, Mass., they are very active in the Boston Anti-Slavery Society and loathe Lucy Stone's bloomer outfit; Jan. 30, Abby Folsom attends Annual Anti-Slavery Meeting at Music Hall in Boston
1854 Plymouth Gas Company is incorporated, homes were supplied with gas for heating;
Oct. 14, Mercy Bisbee Jackson protests at Plymouth Assessors Office for "Taxation without Representation"
1855 Ichabod Morton and other residents drew up a Proposal to ask Selectmen to allow South Plymouth to have its own town, the proposal was defeated; Abby and Zilpha Spooner help conduct a May Fair and Breakfast with all proceeds going toward Progressive Lectures at Davis Assembly Room; Dec. 22, Wendell Phillips was invited to Plymouth to speak in Davis Hall in celebration of the Anniversary of the Landing of the Pilgrims; Mary Grew, daughter of Rev. Henry Grew, visited the home of Mr. and Mrs. Garrison in Boston
1857 Feb. 6, John (Deep Water) Russell died, husband of Deborah Spooner, father of Laura Russell whose manuscript is published as "Laura Russell Remembers: A memoir of living in Plymouth during the Nineteenth Century"; Dred Scott Decision, U.S. Supreme Court rules against Congress having authority to outlaw slavery in
any territory of the United States
1859 Dec. 2, John Brown hanged; Dec. 5, Ephraim Harlow died, abolitionist and Morton friend; Dec. 22, Bourne Spooner, President of Old Colony Anti-Slavery Society, places ad in Old Colony Memorial on upcoming meetings and lists speakers
1860 Feb. 29, Mercy Bisbee Jackson graduates from Boston College; Homeopathy Medicine
1861 American Civil War begins; April, Plymouth Selectmen announce the town will provide for families of men who left to fight in the Civil War; Capt. C. Doten's men were the first in the state to respond for the Union Army, were without provisions for three days on Boston Common, military salary: $6 per month for family and $4 per month for single men; local women helped make the men's uniforms; William Davis helped recruit and traveled to war sites with supplies; May 10, Abby's father
Ichabod Morton dies, he is buried in Plymouth's Oak Grove Cemetery
1862 Sept. 27, OCM publishes Emancipation Proclamation by President Lincoln
1863 Jan. 1, President Lincoln signs Emancipation Proclamation; Feb. 22, William Shaw Russell died, author of "Guide to Plymouth and Recollections

of the Pilgrims" and "Pilgrim Memorials and Guide to Plymouth", husband of Mary Winslow Hayward

1864 George Thompson, the fiery abolitionist, returns to Boston to go on tour and is well accepted

1865 Abby returns to Plymouth to teach at 8 North Street (in the Weston Block); husband Manuel Diaz appears to have disappeared, nothing in print justifies his disappearance; Mary Grew and Margaret (Jones) Burleigh visit Clarks Island as guests of Edward Watson (Mary and Margaret were abolitionists and helped organize American Anti-Slavery Society in Pennsylvania in 1833)

1865 13th Amendment to the U.S. Constitution abolishes slavery; Fredrika Bremer died,

1801-65, feminist and pacifist, Swedish novelist who was admired for her writing and her outspoken anti-slavery sentiments

1867 Mary Elizabeth Preston-Stearns died (1809-67), niece of abolitionist Lydia Maria Childs

1869 July 17, "Uncle" Peter Holmes died, shipmaster for Col. Davis, consort of Sally Harlow

1870 Abby leaves Plymouth, resides in Belmont, Mass., with son Roberto; July 7, Abby's maternal uncle Coomer Weston Jr. died, he was first Capt. of the Standish Guards and Jail Keeper in Plymouth; July 21, Bourne Spooner died, founder of Cordage Co.and abolitionist; the Grimke sisters, Angelina & Sarah, were the first women to tryto vote in Massachusetts, poll keepers did not count the Grimke sister votes

1875 May; Abby's stepmother died, Betsey Holbrook Morton, Ichabod Morton's second wife, the mother of Abby's five brothers: George, Nathaniel, Ichabod, Austin and Howard

1876 Abby gave her first public address to a Congress of Women in Philadelphia, her lecture was on "Characters in Schools" as part of an Anti-Slavery Society gathering, attended by Susan B. Anthony; Aug. 8, Abby's Uncle Edward Watson died on Clark Island in Plymouth, Abby helped nurse Uncle Ed while he was sick, he was nicknamed "Lord of The Isle" by the statesman Daniel Webster of Marshfield

1877 July 21, Bourne Spooner died, leaving wife Hannah Bartlett and five sons, he was President of Plymouth Old Colony Anti-Slavery, founder of Plymouth's Cordage Company in 1824, his home is now the Davis Funeral Home in North Plymouth;

Dec. 13, Dr. Mercy Ruggles Bisbe Jackson died, formally of Plymouth, wife of Capt. Daniel Jackson, she was an educator and a homeopathic doctor

Self Guided Tour: Abolitionists of Plymouth

1878 First telephone installed in Plymouth, the use of the telegraph system continued
1879 Old Colony Memorial reported Mrs. A.M. Diaz active for The Pilgrimage Fair in Plymouth; May 24, William Lloyd Garrison died at his daughter's home in New York City
1880 Old Colony Memorial reported Mrs. Diaz spoke in Plymouth about household talk; tax-paying registered women of Plymouth allowed to vote for School Committee, the first time women voted in Plymouth's history; April 14, Abolitionist Rev.Samuel Osgood died; Lydia Maria Francis Childs died, author, abolitionist and reformer
1881-92 Abby was President of Women's Educational and Industrial Union in Boston, lectured on Household Talks and promoted WEIU, lectured for Educational League of Cambridge, President of the Belmont Women's Suffrage League, organized thec women's Christian Socialist Society, became a follower of Edward Bellamy Movement
1882 August, N.B. Spooner dies, consort to Zilpha Spooner, Abby's childhood antislavery friend, Desire's older sister
1884 Mrs. B.G. Eddy wrote admiring article about Abby Morton Diaz, she had heard her lecture for the WEIU; Wendell Phillips died (1811-1884), famous orator and abolitionist
1887 Mary Tyler Peabody Mann died, consort to Horace Mann (first Massachusetts Secretary of Education), sister to Elizabeth Palmer Peabody and Sophia Peabody Hawthorne, Abby's father Ichabod traveled with Horace Mann promoting the building of schools for public education
1891 Feb. 19, Zilpha Harlow Washburn Spooner died, Abby's childhood friend
1892 January, Capt. John Carnes died, a Wellingsley Morton family friend, his twin sons were sketched in Abby M. Diaz' children's books (see obituary)
1893 Lucy Stone died, feminist, suffragist, abolitionist; m. Henry Blackwell whose sisters were Elizabeth and Emily and brother Samuel
1894 Nov. 25, Charles Burton died, consort to Sarah Stephens (cousin to A.M. Diaz), hec was a teacher and later superintendent in Plymouth.
1903 July 19, Benjamin Drew died at 90, writer of "Pens and Types," "The North Side of Slavery," and "Epitaphs of Burial Hill", a teacher in Boston with roots in Plymouth.Frederick Law Olmstead died, toured the southern states to study the effects of slavery on agriculture and wrote, "The Cotton Kingdom" and "The Slave States", father to Frederick Law Olmstead Jr., architect of Plymouth's Training Green
1902 Elizabeth Cady Stanton died, suffragist, organizer and writer

1904 March 31, Abigail Morton Diaz died in Belmont, buried in the Belmont Cemetery.

CPSIA information can be obtained at www.ICGtesting.com
Printed in the USA
BVOW06s0811080416

443127BV00003B/7/P